HORSE TRAINING
with BILGER

Copyright © 2023 Robert Bilger.

All rights reserved. No part of this book may be reproduced, stored, or transmitted by any means—whether auditory, graphic, mechanical, or electronic—without written permission of both publisher and author, except in the case of brief excerpts used in critical articles and reviews. Unauthorized reproduction of any part of this work is illegal and is punishable by law.

ISBN: 979-8-89031-345-4 (sc)
ISBN: 979-8-89031-346-1 (hc)
ISBN: 979-8-89031-347-8 (e)

Because of the dynamic nature of the Internet, any web addresses or links contained in this book may have changed since publication and may no longer be valid. The views expressed in this work are solely those of the author and do not necessarily reflect the views of the publisher, and the publisher hereby disclaims any responsibility for them.

One Galleria Blvd., Suite 1900, Metairie, LA 70001
1-888-421-2397

ROBERT BILGER

My Horse Training experience started in the mid - late 1960's in Arizona; riding with real horsemen that were in their 50's - 60's age wise and had a horse between their legs their entire lives. What they could do with Horses was truly amazing and they did it very quietly and calmly! My first paid job training horses was in 1968 training horses for polo players. After 45+ years training and modifying the behavior of horses, it has become apparent that in order for anyone to be safe and have an excellent experience with the horse they need to have a relationship with the horse that establishes respect, leadership and trust! This can _only_ be accomplished with _boots on the ground_, by anyone that will put forth the time and effort to understand and work _with_ the horse! This guide will teach you a very specific technique that works on every breed of horse, every time and with excellent results. This technique is also the perfect way to start a horse under saddle that has never been ridden! This technique will create the perfect relationship with every horse; regardless breed, age discipline or already being under saddle!

Should you be able to put forth the effort every other day or at least every 3rd day, you will be able to build your relationship and place a new horse under saddle within 30 days.

Should you apply these techniques to a horse that is already under saddle, you will build your relationship and be riding safely within a week.

* * * * * * * *

Most barn owners are not Horse Trainers

Most barn Managers are not Horse Trainers

Most riding Instructors are not Horse Trainers

Most ribbon winners are not Horse Trainers

Most riders that grew up taking lessons are not Horse Trainers

Anyone at any age with a desire to have a horse can be a Horse Trainer!

INDEX

To Achieve the Ultimate Relationship with the Horse Safely, only **Perform these Techniques in Order!**

Understand the Horse 1

Truth About the Horse 3

Handle the Horse 5

The Round Pen 7

Ground Work 9

Establishing a Relationship 11

Free Lunging Techniques 15

Hand Ground Work 17

Finished Hand Ground Work 21

Tacking the Horse 23

Time to Ride 27

Riding out Alone 29

Final Statement and Truth 31

Opinions of this Author/Trainer 33

The Horse and Panic 37

Personal Assistance 39

Practicing the following techniques, anyone that wants to be SAFE and a _Horse Trainer_, Can Be!

UNDERSTAND THE HORSE

The horse is a very intelligent animal that can live free in the wild, adapt to any environment and survive well without any human interference. You need to understand the horse and be willing to work _with_ its raw instinctive behavior in order to develop an excellent working relationship between you and _each_ horse. The horse is very cautious, approaches every situation carefully and does not believe in or trust _any_ situation until it has been proven that it can do so! The horse keeps its world very simple by deciding if whatever is happening is good or bad, if good it remains curious, willing to work and if bad it uses flight to run away. The horse also likes its world black or white, right or wrong with no gray area! The gray area is very confusing to the horse and makes it difficult to focus or understand what is being asked. The horse has the same psychological and emotional process you do and understands being aggressive, submissive, kindness, reward, fear and pain. If you behave in a way that would trigger fear or cause pain _you_ will get a response which may result in injury or could be fatal; especially in a restricted area where the horse cannot use flight to solve the problem! The horse is most comfortable free and in a totally open area where it has the ability to use flight as a solution to anything it sees as a problem. The moment you place a fence around the horse, place it in a paddock, round pen, stall or trailer the fear level in the horse is escalated with each confined area becoming smaller. The most dangerous place to be with a horse that is fearful is a trailer and the second most a stall, especially if it is a Mare with a foal. Pay attention to the height of the horse head at all times, every horse holds its head in a normal relaxed and curious position with the neck line just above being level with the ground. There is some variation to this once you have worked with many breeds however, <u>ALL</u> horses will raise their heads from normal position when concerned and very high when extremely concerned. Horses that hold their heads extremely high raise their tail and blow out hard making a warning sound are on the edge of panic and you should be clear of them unless you have already established a solid relationship with the ability to calm them down!

TRUTH ABOUT THE HORSE

In a herd environment the horse uses body language, body impact, biting and kicking to establish itself within the group. This is learned behavior within the horse world and will always be part of their life forever when not working with a human being! You need to establish respect, leadership and trust in order to be safe and have the horse understand that the herd behavior is <u>not</u> part of working with you. The horse is extremely cautious and suspicious of everything you do until it is <u>proven</u> to be OK. The horse believes that everything below the height of their eyes could be safe and everything above the height of their eyes to be a threat. With this knowledge it is easy to use your height to determine how the horse views you. Short persons such as children are usually seen by the horse as safe, while tall persons are seen as a threat, especially when they raise their hands above their head. You are going to enter a confined space and ask the horse to respond to everything you do both physically and verbally. In the beginning the horse will only understand what you do physically and learn your words and language as the relationship grows. What you do with your entire body and where your focus is with your eyes will immediately mean everything to the horse. In the beginning the horse will have no idea what you are saying verbally until you use the same word or phrase with the same response consistently however; the horse will totally understand the _tone_ in your voice as being aggressive, passive or fearful. ALWAYS remember that working with a horse is exactly like going back to working on a dial up computer! The horse will NEVER respond at 3g, 4g, or 5g speeds and _you_ must progress at the rate the horse allows or _you_ will not be safe!

There are times that you must be more aggressive and possibly use tools to get the horse to respond exactly the way you want however, the aggressiveness on your part needs to match what the horse will allow. ALWAYS remember that if the horse cannot use flight and get far away from you, your aggressiveness if seen as a threat forces the horse to defend itself. The horse can and will hurt you if it views you as a threat! ALWAYS consistently _ask_ the horse to perform the requested task until you achieve it and NEVER believe you can _force_ it to happen. Proceeding with knowledge, understanding and patience will allow you to establish a relationship with each horse and have the horse respect you, view you as a leader and trust you! A horse that has been mistreated, traumatized or allowed to develop bad habits may need a Professional Trainer to recover or correct the issue. Domestically raised horses handled from birth with human touch are easily trained with the techniques that follow. Wild Mustang and Burro off public lands require much more patience and understanding!

HANDLE THE HORSE

When horses meet each other they do it with caution however, immediately go nose-to-nose to smell and determine which one is going to be aggressive! Approach the horse with the same caution that it does you, keep in mind that the first thing the horse wants to do is smell you and that means going nose-to-nose. Offer your hand first slowly, keeping in mind horses do not like sudden fast movements.

When you allow any part of your body close to the horse nose <u>always</u> be prepared to pull back if the horse reaches for you with its lips or teeth. Reaching for you in any way with their teeth is an aggressive test and they are looking to be dominant or above you in the pecking order, a quick flick of your finger at the nose will solve the problem. Your first goal is to be able to halter the horse and lead it around fairly easily, do this in a controlled area such as paddock or arena. In the beginning most horses will not allow any hand contact below the shoulders or hips. If this is the case, wait until after you begin your relationship and training in the round pen as it will be much easier and safer. If the horse allows you to do any hands on touching or grooming prior to the ground work in the round pen take advantage of that. Once you can halter and lead the horse to a round pen, you are ready to begin the process of establishing your relationship and training the horse. Be prepared to learn from the horse, this is a relationship between two different species and with knowledge, understanding and patience will be the most rewarding thing you ever accomplish!

THE ROUND PEN

The round pen is the _most_ important tool that any horse, trainer and rider will ever spend time in! After 45+ years of working _with_ horses there is a very specific size and configuration to achieving your goals completely and in the least amount of time. The diameter should be 60 feet, the height should be 5 feet, and panels should be all the same size and color with no specific entrance gate. The 60 foot diameter allows for acceptable distance between you and the horse during training for both movement of the horse and safety. Even the larger breeds can achieve walk, trot and canter on the rail without stress to the joints. The 5 foot height ensures that the horse will not give serious thought to jumping out when you are being aggressive in asking it to move out and away from you or when being asked to speed up. The panels all being the same size and color gives the horse a constant visual that the rail never ends anywhere. Not having a specific entrance gate ensures that the horse does not have an obstruction or use the gate as a stopping point during training when it believes it has completed enough work.

GROUND WORK

Working with the horse on the ground and in a round pen is the _ONLY_ way to safely establish a working relationship with _each_ horse for several reasons. Most importantly the horse can see you, every movement you make, look in your eyes when necessary and read both your body language and mind set. Wearing a hat with a brim, cap with a bill or sunglasses will greatly extend the time it takes to train the horse! The horse wants and needs to see your eyes which allow it to be sure that you both are still connected and it can trust you. The space in the round pen allows for the horse to do most of the work and you to only work hard when necessary. Everything you are going to do on the ground where the horse can see you will help the horse to trust you later when you are sitting in its blind spot on its back and asking him to allow you to ride while the horse performs your requested tasks. If you are not willing to do the ground work, you should expect not to be safe while riding!

ESTABLISHING A RELATIONSHIP

The sooner you begin working in the round pen on your relationship with any horse the safer both of you will be! Enter the round pen and take the time to lead the horse along the rail with the horse against the rail and you on the inside towards the center. Make 2-3 full circles and then switch going the opposite way, once again the horse on the rail and you on the inside making 2-3 full circles. When you switch direction make sure you keep the horses head on the rail looking out and its tail to the center. This will show the horse what you want him to do and when free lunging with you in the center of the round pen the horse will switch looking away from you and not at you. This is very important in the training process as the horse switching away from you is a submissive and trusting move unlike switching towards and looking at you which is an aggressive move in the horses mind. During this ground work process you are going to do everything with the horse on both sides, leading, lunging, tacking, mounting, etc. so that the horse is always comfortable with you on either side and does not end up with either a preferred or spooky side. Working all tasks from both sides will always allow you to solve any fear issue with the horse when it is afraid of any object while you are leading it from the ground. When you place yourself between horse and the object of concern it will calm the horse as well as keep you from getting run over when the horse spooks, the horse always jumps away from the object of fear! Now you are ready to begin real progress, remove the halter and lead line allowing the horse to be free. Place the halter outside of the round pen and keep the lead line for yourself as a tool to ask and encourage the horse to move away from you. Your goal is to move the horse away from you, getting it to the rail and continue to move forward until you allow it to stop. Use the lead line by swinging it; remember the height you are swinging it at will get a more immediate response from the horse if it is above the height of the horse eye. Use your body by going at the horse and get the horse to move away. You are going to be as aggressive as necessary to move the horse, do so by going directly towards the hip and tail area however, do not get close enough that the horse could reach you by kicking out! If swinging of the lead line high does not move the horse away from you, it is acceptable to throw the line end of the lead towards the butt area making contact if necessary to move the horse off. Once again NEVER get close enough to the horse that it could reach you by kicking out. The goal with free lunging is to use your body, tools and determination in a manner that allows you to get the horse to continually move along the rail, switch direction away from you and perform at a walk, trot and canter in both directions when you ask. Getting the horse to perform without even a halter on teaches the horse to respect you, focus on what _you_ want and believe you are the leader! The ending to the free lunge session that is preferred would be to say "whoa" have the horse stop moving forward and face you; then be asked to come in to you in the center by you motioning with your hand and taking one step back. This will take time and you may need to walk towards the horse a few times and ask it to follow you in with you walking backwards towards the center. Gently placing the lead rope over its neck and having the horse follow you to the center is acceptable once or twice. When the horse ends its free lunging after hearing "whoa", walks directly to you and drops its head _you_ will always be in control of that horse from that day forward with respect, leadership and trust! ALWAYS praise the horse verbally when it is doing as you ask during free lunging and with a light, kind touch on the forehead when it finishes and comes to you!

FREE LUNGING TECHNIQUES

Every horse has its own character and responds differently to being lunged free. Your job is to observe the horse and determine what is necessary to achieve the wanted behavior.

Should the horse cut inside towards you and not be willing to stay on the rail, try moving directly towards the shoulder maintaining that approach line so that the horse moves away from you and to the rail. Again, never get close enough to the horse that it can reach you by kicking out! Only be as aggressive as necessary however, swinging the lead line high during the approach to the shoulder should do the job.

Every attempt should be made to achieve your round pen goals with only your body, eye focus and the lead line. There are horses that require the use of another tool to keep you safe. If the horse is really stubborn or aggressive showing that it may kick you, use a lunge whip with the correct amount of light weight line tied to the end so that you are able to reach the horse from the center of the round pen while it is on the rail. Flip the line at the horse when it cuts inside towards you, touching the horse if necessary to encourage it to stay on the rail. As soon as possible get the horse to perform on the rail without the use of the whip and line.

Getting the horse to switch direction away from you is extremely important! In the beginning the horse may need you to run towards the rail way ahead of its direction and at the same time throw your hand with the lead line high in the air. This will make the horse raise its head and turn away from you switching direction. Use a word such as "switch" when asking for that behavior, this has been found to greatly assist the horse in performing the task more calmly.

As the horse begins to focus on your exact movements, the required effort on your part will be greatly reduced for all tasks. Once the horse begins to completely focus on you, there will be one ear and one eye on you at all times and your actions and movement will become a priority to the horse.

HAND GROUND WORK

At the end of your walk, trot, canter and switching on the rail session, this is the perfect time to perform the _in hand_ close leading work while the horse cools off. Place the halter back on the horse and make sure that it is tight enough to allow your whole hand inside the lower nose band on the bottom however, just loose enough that you are able to make a fist and roll your upper knuckles into the horse lower jaw bone while maintaining hold on the halter. Now you are going to lead the horse with your hand loosely positioned on the lower nose band holding the halter. Remember to allow your hand to move with any head movement that the horse performs naturally during its walk. This will be different depending upon the breed of the horse and the way it moves. Once again place the horse on the rail with your position on the inside towards the center and complete 2-3 circles each way with you always to the inside or center. You will need to develop being comfortable with using both your right and left hand depending upon which side of the horse you are on. Now come off the rail at locations you determine and cut directly across the round pen by gently tapping on the halter in the direction you are turning when making your turns to cut across, same tapping when you reach the rail on the other side and begin to go along the rail again.

Perform this leading and cutting across both directions and switching sides. You may want to add a verbal command here of left or right each time you tap on the halter, which will greatly help when you first ride and are teaching the horse to move left and right off of the bit. Many times during your walk use _whoa_ immediately rolling your knuckles into the horse lower jaw bone, making sure to release when the horse stops. You are simulating a stop and the horse should stop quickly in place, not pull you forward and not raise its head.

Many times after the whoa ask the horse to _back_ using the word, rolling your knuckles into the lower jaw bone with a tapping motion and having the horse back straight up a few steps. It may be necessary to place a finger or two in the horse chest area just either side of the breast bone and gently push back while rolling your knuckles and saying back. Backing is EXTREMELY difficult for the horse as its mind set based upon _raw instinct_ is to NEVER back up as this is a completely submissive move! It is extremely important that the horse understands that when working with you it is OK to back up, the horse should do so easily on command and remember to praise the horse greatly each time it backs for you! The backing upon command reinforces your position as both a leader and the horse learns it is OK to be submissive with you when asked. Being able to back the horse on command from the ground and later from the saddle is EXTREMELY important!! This allows you to have the horse be immediately submissive, focus on you and will keep you in control in _ALL_ spooky situations both leading and under saddle.

FINISHED HAND GROUND WORK

When you have successfully <u>Established Your Relationship</u>, used your <u>Free Lunging Techniques</u> and completed your <u>Hand Ground Work</u>; you will have an EXTREMELY willing partner that *respects* you, looks at you as a *leader* and *trusts* you! At the point which you can enter the round pen with this horse, remove the halter and have 3 sessions in a row, during 3 separate time frames go perfectly the way you ask covering all three of the above practices You are now ready to add tack!

TACKING THE HORSE

Enter the round pen, remove halter-lead rope, have a very short walk, trot canter session both ways and ask the horse to finish and come in to you. Place the halter and lead line back on, you are now going to introduce the horse to a pad, saddle, cinch it up and leave the stirrups hanging down. Remember to perform this introduction at a pace that the horse is comfortable with and has time to accept. If you reach to put each item on the horses back and it steps away, go back to the horse nose allowing it time to smell and touch the item and then proceed again. While holding the horse loosely with the lead rope have the horse see and touch the stirrups on both sides, then gently touch him with the stirrups on each side and end by holding them out and allowing them to swing in to the horse body until he no longer flinches. Walk the horse around the rail both ways with the stirrups free and then make some turns crossing thru the middle. If all this goes well and the horse is not fearful of the stirrups remove the lead line and free lunge walk, trot and canter in both directions. Most horses will trust you and think nothing of the stirrups moving around and making contact as they will be focused on working for you.

Occasionally you will get a horse that accelerates and bucks a few times in response to the stirrups making contact with the body however, in most instance they settle down very quickly and focus on you. Once the horse settles down and has accepted the saddle with stirrups occasionally making contact with its body, add the breast strap and back cinch or strap if you are going to ride western. Free lunge again to be sure the horse is accepting of it. Now introduce the horse to a bit, bridle and reins making sure to secure the reins to the front of the saddle or mane in a manner that allows for free movement of the horses head while working however, not long enough to get caught on anything. It is very important to position the bit at a location in the horse mouth that is the most comfortable! This location is ¾ - 1 inch from the front edge of the back teeth in the horse mouth. Once again free lunge both directions walk, trot and canter. The horse may mouth the bit for a short time however, should accept the bit fairly soon and focus on the job with the lunging. Pay attention to the height of the horse head, if he has accepted all of the tack and is very calm, it will be a good time to practice mounting. If you are not an experienced trainer the mounting practice should be done with another person holding the horse. Allow the horse to pay attention to what you are doing, place your foot in the stirrup and bring yourself up into a position where you are standing on one leg with your other leg next to it free. You want to go up and down several times without swinging your leg over. Go the opposite side and do the same thing going up and down several times. If this is going smoothly it is now time to go up, swing your leg over slowly, place your outside foot in the stirrup and relax in the saddle. Let the horse know that you are relaxed and trusting it. Do this several times and go to the other side repeating the same procedure. It is important that the horse understands and is able to allow mounting from both sides. This should be the end of this session and the horse should receive much praise from you while you remove the tack. Constant praise as each task is completed with the horse staying calm is highly recommended!

TIME TO RIDE

Enter the round pen, remove halter-lead line, have a short free lunging session to get the horse focused on you, finish with the horse coming to you and dropping its head placing the halter and lead line on. Introduce to the pad, saddle, breast strap, back strap if necessary, bit, bridle and reins. Secure the reins and free lunge the horse making sure it has once again accepted all of the tack. Use another person to hold and proceed with mounting from each side only a couple of times and then mount and relax. When you feel the horse relax and the head position is at a normal height ask the horse to move forward and walk with someone leading it. Make 2-3 circles each way near the rail with some switching. If the horses head remains relaxed and the height is normal pick up the reins and with very light pressure ask the horse to stop and back up.

Should the horse remain calm, with head height normal, have your helper go to the center of the round pen and begin riding at a walk. Enjoy each circle, switch when you want, stop and back up occasionally and then begin crossing thru the middle and turning both ways when reaching the other side. Always use as little pressure as possible on the reins and bit, use a tapping motion on the side of the bit that you want the horse to turn towards and only pull back and hold with both sides when you want the horse to stop, making sure to release all pressure the moment the horse stands still.

Use the word _stand_ when stopping and releasing pressure on the reins and bit. If you want the horse to remain standing for any period of time _drop_ the reins on the horse neck. Repeat until the horse stands until such time as you pick up the reins, say walk or touch the horse side with the stirrups. This would be a good time to end the session unless you are extremely confident the horse could handle a trot and you are experienced with posting in the saddle to make it smooth in the first trotting experience with a rider on. Proceed with more riding sessions in the round pen until you are able to walk, trot, canter, stop and back up when asked with a calm horse and head in a relaxed normal position. When both you and horse are confident and ready, open the round pen and begin riding with another horse with you. For the first few rides and always when riding in a new area, take a horse with experience and confidence in the area you are going as a companion. This will keep you and the new horse safe until you are ready to attempt riding out alone.

RIDING OUT ALONE

It is always advisable to use a companion horse with any new riding out on trail or park riding. If you have performed all of the handling, ground work, round penning and starting personally; trust your instincts and your read of the horse. Once again the height of the horses head will always be a sign of how much the horse is concerned and if there is a problem; stop, back up and get the horse to drop its head and focus on you before proceeding. While out with the companion horse practice leaving that horse and coming back together, go away until the horse becomes concerned then come back together. Making the distance farther and then being able to ride out of site and come back is your goal. When ready to venture out alone from the barn, tack and walk the horse out on the ground until you are out of sight of the barn, mount and go for a ride. Always be willing to go as far as you can without asking the horse to go farther than it will trust you to take it. Just like in the beginning of establishing your relationship, be willing to work with what the horse is comfortable with and will allow!

Each time you go out alone the horse will trust you to go farther until there is no limit and it totally trust you as its partner and companion. This is the best and most free feeling in the world to be able to ride out alone, just you and your horse! The _only_ way to be safe riding out alone in a new area or on trail is by completing the techniques in this training process. Not having established respect, leadership and trust is taking a HUGE personal risk! Some horses are so fearful of being out alone that it may be necessary to have a professional _Horse Trainer_ be slightly more aggressive and prove to the horse that it has the confidence to be ridden out alone.

FINAL STATEMENT AND TRUTH

The Horse is Capable of any Riding Style or Venue its Only Limitation is the _Rider_!

Most riders will never experience the trust, emotional and spiritual rewards of training and riding out alone with a horse. This is a result of not believing they have the ability to understand the horse, perform the ground work, earn its respect, become a leader and develop the trust that is necessary to be a full partner and be safe riding in the outdoor world of trails, parks, cross country and competition. Hiring a trainer to start the horse and/or ride it out in the discipline you are going to ride in _does not_ establish _you_ as respected or a leader under saddle with that horse! Regardless of whether or not the horse has already been under saddle and ridden; performing the entire training process between _you_ and _each_ horse you ride will allow you to be SAFE and experience what the horse has to offer. _You_ will be respected by the horse, a leader in the horses mind, have the ultimate relationship and be _safe_ with that horse. Your riding from that moment forward will be the most rewarding possible, with each ride getting more enjoyable! Riding any horse without performing the training process personally means that _you_ are willing to take all of the risks associated with riding a horse that only someone else has an established relationship with this is NOT intelligent!

OPINIONS OF THIS AUTHOR/ TRAINER

he horse will allow anyone with the understanding and knowledge to work with it!

The horse is a highly intelligent animal and spends its entire life adapting to its surroundings.

The horse is capable of learning any language however, only in single words or short phrases.

The horse will always be cautious and only accept things that are <u>proven</u> to be trustworthy.

The horse should *never* be trained with treats however, *always* be rewarded at the end of any training session or riding with apples, carrots and a small amount of extra grain to offset the exercise performed!

Picking up and cleaning hoofs should be performed each time you work or ride the horse! Attempt this after you have performed your round pen work and established a solid relationship. This is the ultimate test of trust with the horse and will allow the horse to remain calm when being trimmed or in need of shoes. If it is difficult to do all 4 hoofs each time you work or ride the horse, there are very specific techniques that will get this done.

Make sure you accomplish this task or get assistance from a professional! The individual that trims your horse will be safe and thank you!

The horse visually does not understand the 3rd dimension! A wet spot, puddle, creek, river or lake could not have a bottom. A black spot, sidewalk, driveway, road or parking lot could be a huge hole they will fall in. A hole such as wash stall drain, road side drain or culvert may have something jump out and eat them.

The horse has no way of ever understanding why it is sold or relocated and needs time to process the move!

The horse when moved should be allowed a minimum of a week to settle in to the new location, realize and accept a new routine before being ridden.

The horse should be allowed at minimum 2-3 days of being near the new horses it will be turned out with and during this time there should be a fence or gate between for protection of all horses.

The new horse should be introduced to the new group by the individual with the most experience with that group. There is a specific procedure that works extremely well for this, eliminating or minimizing damage.

The horse will take at least 30 days to believe this could be a new permanent location and home.

The horse will take a full 12 months to totally accept a new owner and/or new location; in the horses mind one unit of experience means that it arrived or began a new relationship in a particular season and came full circle back to that season.

The horse will never accept a new rider by that rider just climbing on! A new rider is always extremely concerning to the horse and sets up both rider and horse for failure! There is a specific short introduction procedure for this that works prior to climbing on.

Due to the structure and development of the spine, no horse should be placed under saddle and be worked in a trot or canter prior to age 3 regardless of how large it is.

The horse does have a rider weight limitation that should always be respected; 10% of the horse weight for cross country or jumping, 15% for all work related discipline riding or trail and 20% maximum for walking flat work or flat trail riding!

The horse will always be willing to work for <u>any</u> individual that will take the time to understand the horse, the raw instinctive behavior and work within the limitations that behavior!

THE HORSE AND PANIC

The horse has 3 major senses that will always place it on the edge of panic: (1) Hearing something it has never experienced before or that sound recalls a negative incident, (2) Smelling something it has never experienced before or the smell recalls a negative incident and (3) seeing something it has never experienced before or that sight recalls a negative experience. If you are the first person to lead or ride a horse during any of these new experiences; you had better have a solid relationship with respect, leadership and trust or it will always end negatively!

You MUST have the complete Knowledge, Respect, Leadership and Trust of <u>each</u> Horse that you ride before ever riding outside of the controlled area both you and the horse are comfortable in!

PERSONAL ASSISTANCE

Any individual at any age that wants a horse and is willing to learn this entire training process, can become an excellent Horse Trainer and Rider! This entire training process and even more techniques can be experienced personally from this author and trainer by scheduling a training session. Visit www.HorseTrainingwithBilger.com or email Horsemanusa@gmail.com for more information on a program for you or a group.

My personal goal after 45+ years training horses is to pass this knowledge on to the persons that are willing to truly understand, appreciate the horse and respect the absolutely incredible gift they are willing to share with those that put in the time, effort and treat the horse fairly!

The rewards cannot be described, they must be experienced!

www.ingramcontent.com/pod-product-compliance
Lightning Source LLC
LaVergne TN
LVHW051041070526
838201LV00067B/4883